Jersey's open mic poetry collective **La Poèt'tie** (pronounced Poet Tea) is an inclusive and supportive group where poetry is celebrated and appreciated.

Our first anthology **SMALL ISLAND BIG DREAMS** is a diverse selection of original work from a wonderfully eclectic group.

Sponsored By

First published as paperback by Juliette Hart, September 2022
The Grey Havens, 3 Grainville Court, Bagatelle Road, St Saviour, Jersey JE2 7GA

ISBN 978-1-9998482-1-7

Printed by Bigwoods Premier Printers, designed by Lawrence Chay.

Dear Ana
Thank you for coming
to Jersey again !

SMALL ISLAND
BIG DREAMS

Poetry from Jersey collective La Poèt'tie

I hope you enjoy the poems
about my Mum, and Dad ! (Pages 28/29)

All the best
Juliette x

FOREWORD

It all began with a poetry slam.

In 2018 Stefan Le Marquand and I attended an event at which Farrago Poetry merged with the Jersey Festival of Words, where pizza was served and poetry performed against the backdrop of Market Street's ornate gates, beneath bunting and the glow of streetlights. It was illuminating. A spark was ignited.

We had occasionally met at the Curiosity Coffee Shop to casually discuss poetry and, in the enthusiasm of the moment, Stefan suggested that there may be an appetite for more regular meetings.

Jersey's open mic poetry collective La Poèt'tie was founded by us at the start of 2019. The name, meaning 'a collective of poets / a place where poetry is made / a place where poets gather', was created during a meeting with Geraint Jennings, poet and promoter of Jèrriais.

Our ethos was simple - La Poèt'tie would provide an inclusive and supportive environment where poetry both old and new could be celebrated and appreciated with applause.

Since then we've heard everything from sonnets to limericks, haiku to odes; poems which have made us think, connect, laugh, cry, understand; poetry from classic, contemporary and emerging poets; verse from all over the world, in many languages and in translation; and original poems from those attending.

We believed that some of the original work shared during meetings deserved to reach a wider audience, so I invited our regular attendees to submit their contributions for this, our first anthology.

It's a diverse selection from a wonderfully eclectic group. We cover all ages, backgrounds and experiences - for many this is the first time they have been published. From grands rêves to peccadilloes to dandelions, if our poetry has inspired you perhaps you'll seek out, and join, the next La Poèt'tie meeting?

I'll end with the words of one of our contributors:

Being part of La Poèt'tie is great because we get to hear so many different genres and there is no criticism, just encouragement!

Mèrcie bein des fais
JULIETTE HART

CONTENTS

Contents Continued ...

JÈRRI PRÊCHE (JERSEY SPEAKS)

Commissioned by Highvern for World Poetry Day
21 March 2019

p'tite ville et grands rêves

small town and big dreams
inspiration evolves and ignites

from southern beaches and bustle
the seagull flies
follow us...northward
concrete falls away
to natural beauty
Jersey speaks

Jèrri prêche

words seep into the earth
fields are punctuated with growth
consonants consolidate
in granite cliffs and conglomerate
vowels eddy on sand
in air

flowing from ripple to wave to shore
water finds its language: the voice of an island

la vouaix d'eune île

By Stefan Le Marquand and Juliette Hart
Jèrriais translation by Geraint Jennings

HANNAH
CHERRINGTON-HALL

I'm a primary school educator with a degree in English Literature. At age 9, my first poem was published in the Hullabaloo! Gtr Manchester Vol 1.

During university studies I was inspired by the Romantic era of British poetry and discovered my best-loved poet, William Wordsworth.

I aspire to continue to read, write and listen to poetry as a community.

A LOVE THAT IS TRUE

Memories remain clear when told by two,
Experiences are greater when shared with you.
Desires are fierce with another in mind,
Decisions together made quick and defined.
Beside you I am strong, I am bold,
The world I see in pink hues and rose gold.

It is not that we are two halves of a whole,
But two wholes, both great and of similar soul.
I add to you, and you add to me,
As we bring out the best for all to see.
You see it in me, and I see it in you,
Your power, your beauty, a love that is true.

THE UNKNOWN

Anxiety rising through my chest,
A shortness of breath beneath my breast.
The sight of it all leaves me confused,
My confidence diminished; my ego bruised.
Looking back, I feel regret,
Frustration leads me to upset.
How could it be this was my choice?
That I spoke up and used my voice?
But a fool I was to be so brave,
For in this moment, I cannot be saved.
If I let it be, fear will consume,
It's closing in, walls of a tomb.

"This cannot be my fate", I wallow,
Lost today and still tomorrow.
If I want change, I must persist,
Pessimism and self-doubt resist!
Familiarise myself with the unknown,
Learn its ways until it feels like home.
Determination and belief were what it cost,
To free myself from feeling lost.

WHEN WE WERE THREE

Before we were four, we were three.
Before you, there was only me.
An only child with all the love,
A mother and father could muster up.
No toys to share, no pulling hair,
no uninvited guest.
I'd make my choice, they'd hear my voice,
I was priority.

Then YOU, with your chubby cheeks and chunky thighs,
Stole their attention, diverted their eyes.
OH, how they would gaze over you...
Green with jealousy I grew!
And what a monkey you made of me,
I, singing, dancing foolishly.
All to gain a second look,
a moment more of what you took.

TO FEEL ALIVE

I moved into a house that sat by a lake,
I moved to a country whose language I couldn't speak.
I moved my feet in a dance between lovers,
I moved on, with a touch from another.
I moved forward, grew up, grew tall, grew fat,
I moved backwards, regressed, relapsed, slipped back.
"Move on", they said, "what's next?" "New chapter!",
So I sat still, moved my mind, thought deeper and harder.

I was present, listened to the sounds of the earth,
Smelt the roses, saw the colours, tasted the flavours of the world.
Felt the sand between my toes, and the sunlight as it rose.
But I could not stop moving for long,
Ants in my pants, wiggly worm.
The world kept spinning; the days came in turn.
Days pass, months go by, years fly.
But we do it all to feel alive.

CATHERINE COLLIN

It has been over two years since poetry found me hiding in a dark place; I was nearing 19 years old when poetry became my comfort blanket and emotional outlet.

I'm very grateful that I discovered how to write in my own way, and hope that I continue to write for a very long time.

NEVER PRETTY

Fat body, skinny body, never shed the hate body.
Ugly body, pretty body, this one takes the cake body.
Balancing the plate body, biological trait body –
I'm fed up of counting bodies, can't we just stop?

JUST A BUNCH OF KIDS

When she walked into this spirited crowd,
Controlled by comets shooting about,
It was to blink at a moment in history:
Those trading distilled drink for solid memory.

Those whom she met were better –
Sardine-dancing, sticky shoes-type better –
Hardships-drowned, back pocket-frown fetter.
Gnawing upon gritty adulthood cash –
Spending notes from the social stash.

But each weekend saw the same scene:
The dispirited crowd aftermath scene.
Is there anything that screams empty soul:
Comet kids in Friday night's black hole?

The overbearing darkness of the crowd
Had her running away from the desperate shroud.
Cool kids, like remote dying stars,
Casting supernova light at the bar –
But then it's all over: brain dead superstars.

FORBIDDEN, BUT...

My heart is haunted
With his melody snaking
In the sand dunes;
His name sweeping
Past my ears.
He is a downward dream
Sliding under my feet, and I stagger
Towards the threshold
I want to claim as mine;
It has his face, his hands,
His escape.

All of it is him: the sizzle
On my arms when there is no sun;
The pressure
In my ears, though I am closest
To the ground;
The sordid choice
That drips like blood
From my skin.

Do I dare?

ANYONE AND NO ONE

At the back of the corner shop,
Sweet Red fell down in the dark.
Hollywood red lip, red dress,
Bare hips, tights ripped –
Then the headlines wouldn't stop:
A story of walking home from the park.

CIGARETTE LIGHT

Cradled lighter in my hands,
As though I'm holding our wedding bands;
The soft burning to the touch:
It must be why I miss you so much.

The flicker, the fire, the fuel caged in metal;
It's a wonder you saw me like a petal,
When I so sweetly crushed the colour from our lives,
And betrayed the foolish light in your eyes.

You paid for eternity;
I put a deposit in your finite pocket,
So dreamily, as though I could already see
The dreams you'd have of me, because I was not
Where you thought I'd be.

My presence you curated in a slideshow of memories,
In our museum of the exhausted centuries;
Though we had only met that one night
Outside the bar, and I've archived the fossils
You mistake for scars.

That cigarette we shared was charity:
I am blameless in your decision to marry me.
Although, these years gone, I wish
I had said yes, if the life promised
To me, could be without regret.

NIKKI CRAIG

I was an ordinary Jersey child, always seeking, leading a colourful life from childhood into womanhood. Now I'm approaching midlife 'breakthrough', 'crisis' far too negative a word for my journey.

Through the years I've used diaries and creative writing to process and sift through the layers of personal and spiritual growth.

I'm a loving mother of three beautiful boys.

THE SAVIOUR

Through the shadows of despair,
is the depth of love.
When you feel life is not fair,
the saviour is there.
How time disappears through the dark,
when you slip into the shadows unbeknown.
There is no fun, nor lark,
just the deep lonely unknown.
Until life can sink no further,
you listen to the inside groan.
Only to awaken,
only to see the light,
only to reach out,
and, behold, the saviour is there,
warm, loving, inviting,
the depth of nurturing love and care.

MARRIAGE

Marriage is...
Marriage is comforting
Marriage is suffocating
Marriage is nourishing
Marriage is limiting
Marriage is loving
Marriage is enduring
Marriage is nurturing
Marriage is cold
Marriage is warmth
Marriage is lonely
Marriage is holding
Marriage is...

MOTION

Even in peaceful sleep the mind moves,
flux and flow all around us as we lay,
dreams escaping as they may.
Even in moments of stillness,
time ticks, each beat doesn't miss
every second of every day, hearts beating, clocks ticking.

Life around us forever flowing,
flowers growing, leaves blowing.
Work or resting, moving continues,
the 'Journey of Life', one's muse.
Ageing, weakening, day by day growing old,
change continues, moving towards our destiny of moss and mould.
Nature, the oceans, stars, the planets,
from copulation, conception, to birth,
evolving on a personal journey to find our worth.

Until death.

Does the moving stop then, may I ask?
I wonder, is that when it comes to a halt?
When the heart stops at its final fault?
No, says the soul –
The spirit moves on to its next journey and beyond,
where the mystery of life continues to wave its magic wand!

CONVEYOR BELT

Life flows like a cascade of water,

light shines through the smothering veil.

Don't be tempted to follow like a sheep, so pale,

faking security with bricks and mortar.

MY PLACE

Life is like the tide with its ebb and flow,
the full moon affecting me with its almighty blow.
I go within and overthink,
to feel, to cry, to see my kink.
Drawn to a place with many memories,
somewhere to hide from my worries.

I came many a time to weep,
burying myself in a conscious sleep.
A place for me to sit with inner peace,
where my ancestors have a spiritual lease.

Listening to my moon song,
being held by you did not feel wrong.
I love it here, a place for me,
my place where nature meets the sea.
Hearing the sound of a car, a birdsong not far,
the breeze a blowing, whispers its knowing.

With every thought the shedding of tears,
simply sitting and feeling my fears.
Knowing not having you causes this pain,
but allows a smile as I embrace my memory lane.

JULIETTE HART

Jersey has always influenced and inspired me with its compact diversity and living history, though recent writing has been impacted by the pandemic.

My poems have appeared in many anthologies, and in 2017 I published the pamphlet Reflections of D-Day.

Much of my work records memories of family and friends - it's a preservation of love on the page.

THE FOOTLING PATH

Why waste emotion worrying, why care
about the path extending out of sight?
Each step you take to get from here to there
will not affect new day or dark of night.
The Earth goes on regardless of its fate,
it does not fear a fall, cry tears of rain,
the course of sun and moon is never late,
tides surge, retreat, then surge, retreat again.

How swift the seasons slip away with ease,
so unaware of how the wind will blow,
as blossom fades and fruit grows ripe on trees,
the leaves give way to scatterings of snow.
How still you stand with water all around:
a way forward will, tread by tread, be found.

RISE TO THE SURFACE

The glass is half-full: positives rise to the surface
otherwise what would be the point?
If it were not for the pandemic
multiple fractures from a fall
forty years of diabetes
Dad's heart attack
and distance
from my only sibling
I would remember 2020 for
four bursts of blooming wisteria
a month in my childhood home with Mum
the longest curliest hair since I was sixteen
and my coral-anniversary-husband
learning to cook comfort food
Our son sat in the porch
we talked for hours
his back against
the glass
the glass
between us
and the darkness
My glass is half-full:
positives rise to the surface
otherwise what would be the point?

ORNITHOLOGY, AND LESSONS IN NURTURE

1. Learned Behaviour

That first morning, with Dad not there,
I was the one left standing
as Mum stepped up
into his garden.

I raised my eyes to the sky, dismissive
as she wiped clean the birdbaths
and fussily refilled, fresh
and cool, twice a day.

In the centre of the plot
five feeders swung:
totemic protein-packers
for the little birds.

I'll wean her off these tasks
I thought airily, the sacks of seeds
and nuts toppling in the greenhouse,
that rag rinsed and wrung out on the line.

But within a week
I was on the phone ordering
pellets of suet, then wearing Dad's
jacket to serve the birds their breakfast:

waiting
at the window,
enthralled with the storm
of feathers, the squall and rush of descent.

ORNITHOLOGY, AND LESSONS IN NURTURE

2. The Last Bank Holiday Before Christmas

Dad has been sanding down the workshop,
undercoating in steel grey, in his eighty-eighth year.

The brushstrokes don't give away the tremors
of myocardial infarction which shook
our lives, three months ago.

He leans back, to admire the job. Tomorrow
he'll mix remnants of gloss paint
to an echo of racing green.

Mum, tiny and bird-like,
attends the flower beds, removing
each weed and twig, sifting upturned stones.

She flits out of sight to make
a pot of tea, returns with saucers
rattling, a slice of cake on a plate to share.

Next month is their blue sapphire anniversary:
sixty-five years of tending, nesting, conservation.

ASANA ON THE EDGE OF THE DUNES

In memory MFL

A solitary tree inclines towards the road, roots
scramble-holding sandy soil as trunk
and boughs limber and flex.

> In summer we met close
> to here on our first evening out since Covid,
> not knowing that it would be our last, as two couples.
> Ordering scallops, the lobster, I said next time
> I'd choose the cheapest thing on the menu.
> Our evening was altogether priceless.

We meet today at the southern curve of the bay, where dunes compress
and the slowly shifting mat of flora reaches
the café, tipping towards decking.

We sit around three mugs.
She says the cat
keeps bringing gifts -
a lizard on the doormat
a goldfinch at the foot of the stairs
a tiny rabbit wedged behind the printer.

> Completely balanced
> through lockdown
> we became
> focussed:
> Yogic
> Zen

> After nightfall we'd stood
> in the car park in
> Vrikshasana.
> He, perfectly still,
> in the dark shining,
> smiling and confident
> as always, but as we said
> Goodbye, he scantly swayed,
> just a shadow touch, a murmuration.

As we pass, we acknowledge
the solitary tree, scramble-holding,
her limber boughs flexing, finding balance.

DAY TRIP TO THE FIRST DARK SKY ISLAND IN THE WORLD

We're back home
where our birdsong
is the dirge of traffic

where beetles lack
the colour, carapace
and exotic grace
of jewelled scarabs

where our roses do not
pillow lemon-scented,
diamond-dewed,
in the afternoon.

Less is more, on Sark,
but we had to leave
before incandescence.

GERAINT JENNINGS

I was born in 1966 in Saint Helier, have twice won the Grand Prix for a short story in Norman, translated Alice's Adventures in Wonderland and Through the Looking-Glass into Jèrriais, had poems selected as set pieces for the Jèrriais section of the Jersey Eisteddfod, been commissioned to write poems for many occasions, and regularly perform poetry, both classic and my own.

ÊGRÎNFLIÉE

San fro d'fliambe fliottait l'țou
    d'ses tchiêsses, jutchie là-haut

sus la carre d'l'aveugl'ye tou;
    et l'dragon soûffliait caud

en d'ssous d'mes rouoges êcrèdes
    comme j'avanchais. Ma chai

êteuchinnait. Et raide
    d'san craquelébrède, j'en tchai

dans l'flias d'san feu dé d'si.
    Ma coue à didget chôl'ye,

ma pé d'grupé roûssit,
    ma langue froutchie catouôle...

Nos embraiches en soussinnent,
    j'ligouaîsons en dragons:

mé, caûffé - lyi, en souinne.
    J'l'aveins - mes grîns sont trons.

SCRATCHED

Her flame-dress floated round
                   her thighs, perched up there

on the blind tower's corner;
                   and the dragon blew hot

under my red scales
                   as I advanced. My flesh

spattered. And stiff
                   from her flouncing, I fall down

into the hollowness of her desire-fire.
                   My spiked tail swings,

my stony skin singes,
                   my forked tongue tickles...

Our embraces smoulder,
                   we fondle as dragons:

me, heated - her, in heat.
                   I reach for her - my claws are blunt.

TÉN ASSINNE, MAD'MOUAÎSELLE

Tén assinne, Mad'mouaîselle, rigu'thait un fliottîn dg'ièrs,
rêvilyis au solé et douothant d'or tes louêmes.
Tes vailes voltil'yent ès côtes; les cartchaîthons d'vailièrs
clyinn'tent dé corps et couronnes escliavés pouor ta dgiême.

Mad'mouaîselle, escliave-mé et j'portéthai tes fièrs,
et fo souos tan pouver, encafoté d'tes mains,
mén av'nîn s'sa tes d'mains et j'èrnonch'chai mes hièrs,
et toute ma libèrté n'mé sèrvitha d'aut' rein.

N'y'étha pon d'vent en mé, sans qué j'sais hors d'haleine;
tan solé né s'lève pon si jé n'veins pon ni t'sèrs;
tes frégates frangu'thont l'ieau à la sîl'ye dé ma couenne;
tu n'éthas pon d'assinne si jé n'rigue pon tes sièrs.

36

YOUR DAWN, LADY

Your dawn, Lady, would rig a flotilla of eyes,
woken in sunshine and daubing your waves with gold.
Your sails flutter at the coasts; the cargoes of sailing boats
blink with bodies and wreaths enslaved for your tithe.

Lady, enslave me and I will wear your fetters,
and mad under your power, blindfolded by your hands,
my future will be your tomorrows and I'll renounce my yesterdays,
and all my liberty will be of use to me no longer.

There won't be any wind in the sea that's me, without my being out of breath;
your sun does not rise if I neither come nor serve you;
your frigates will welt the wave-crest of my skin;
you will have no dawn if I don't rig your evenings.

The death of Diana Rigg in 2020 set me thinking about her performance in
On Her Majesty's Secret Service, and her character's ironic recital of lines of poetry
to distract the villain. Those lines, starting

"Thy dawn, O Master of the World, thy dawn
For thee the sunlight creeps across the lawn
For thee the ships are drawn down to the waves .."

were an adaptation of part of the play "Hassan" by James Elroy Flecker (1882-1915).
In my turn, I used these verses as a starting point to play on language, words and
themes from the two versions, and, in tribute, on the surname Rigg.

BURNS HORS LES BORNES

À ces sé ch'est la Séthée d'Burns:
j'soummes en bouaisson et hors les bornes,
nou bait, nou brait, nou balivèrne
en contant des bliues et des bouonnes...

Coumme à la breune dé niet j'brouons
du brueûtîn, et l'fronmy en fliambe:
j'faîthons du flianné, j'nos en bèrne
des cheins tchi n'baivent ni fout' ni bran...

En contant des bliues et des bouonnes,
j'soummes en bouaisson et hors les bornes
à ces sé, ch'est la Séthée d'Burns:
nou bait, nou brait, nou balivèrne...

Quand tu'éthas hèrchi ma brîseûthe,
tu'en saithas mus, au mains un brîn:
la rueûthie l'travèrs d'la bruëthe
né f'tha pon d'bein - j'nos abrévons...

Nou bait, nou brait, nou balivèrne
en contant des bliues et des bouonnes:
à ces sé ch'est la Séthée d'Burns,
j'soummes en bouaisson et hors les bornes...

Ès cheins tchi brîngent eune bouonne boutée,
tchi gângnent dé l'or, d'l'argent, du bronze:
lus j'vaux volent - l's ânes vont mus bâtés -
et j'soummes brînguesîngues pouor l'amour d'Burns...

J'soummes en bouaisson et hors les bornes:
en contant des bliues et des bouonnes,
nou bait, nou brait, nou balivèrne
à ces sé - ch'est la Séthée d'Burns...

BURNS OUT OF BOUNDS

This evening it's Burns Night:
we're boozed up and out of bounds,
gulping, yelping, yarning,
telling tall tales out of the blue...

At twilight we ferment
chatter to make the whisky flame:
flanneling, and flouting
those who don't drink a damn drop...

Telling tall tales out of the blue,
we're boozed up and out of bounds
this evening, it's Burns Night:
gulping, yelping, yarning...

When you've walked a mile in my shoes,
you'll know better, at least a bit.
Rushing through the heather
won't do any good - we fuel ourselves with drink...

Gulping, yelping, yarning,
telling tall tales out of the blue:
this evening it's Burns Night,
we're boozed up and out of bounds...

To those who dash a good distance,
who win gold, silver or bronze:
their horses fly - donkeys go best laden -
and we're sozzled for the sake of Burns...

We're boozed up and out of bounds:
telling tall tales out of the blue,
gulping, yelping, yarning
this evening   it's Burns Night...

[DÊ-OUÔLEZ L'HÔLOUOGE ET DÊCOMPTEZ L'S HEUTHES!]

Dê-ouôlez l'hôlouoge et dêcomptez l's heuthes!
Dêcachiz l's adgulles; qu'les b'sées lus dêpengent!
L'av'nîn va sus l'âge et l'achteu s'êtchoeuthe;
v'là l'vièr Papa Temps tchi tchait en êfange.

l' r'dote, raîque des miettes dé minnutes topinnent;
et sans sa note, la marche du temps sonne quas.
Les heuthes dêsonnent, dêsaîsonnées à sinne
dé jeu – quandi qu'les cliochièrs pâssént lé pas.

Atout des âges, l'engrénage sé clioge;
l's adgulles lus piquent dans la vive chai
du grand hôlouogi tchi bouoge
d'un pas d'entèrrement, fraid
coumme pouaîson. L'hôlouoge
êp'sonne l'heuthe mais
qu'ou s'dêlouoge
et vaie
rouoge.

[UNPICK THE CLOCK AND COUNT DOWN THE HOURS!]

Unpick the clock and count down the hours!
Pull out the hands; let the weights come unhung!
The future's aging and the now's disheartened;
Old Grandfather Time is falling senile.

He's losing his grip, only bits of minutes spin;
and without his note, the march of time's discordant.
The hours unchime, out of season at day-
-break - while belfries kick the bucket.

The clockwork is clogged with the ages;
the clock hands stick into the quick
of the great clockmaker, at
his funereal pace,
poison-cold. The clock
spurs the hour soon
as it strays
and sees
red.

PÉGASE EN MÉTA

Jutchi ès grîns d'la leune, j'èrgarde les dous ès veues,
un mitheux êtailé d'constellâtions en bas.
Lé nièr est picoté dé dgiamants ès dgieux,
eune trésôr'rie brûlante, eune fliambée d'falbalas.

Mèrtchure, les ailes ès g'vil'yes, né tcheurt pon d'itelle ièrre;
Nepteune, la mé montante, né chôl'ye pon l'ochéan
au pas qué j'pilonne l'air souos l'ciel, par d'ssus d'la tèrre -
mes engambées gavèlent les êmânues du vent,

ches couotheurs d'l'horizon, les dragons ès êcrèdes
d'or tchi teurtil'yent la niet. Châque pas d'galop d'Pégase
saque des êparts dé feu. Lé méta d'goutte en dréd-
-illets qué Vultchain forge dé cliapes dé feunque et d'gaz.

Les fliaues sont câsuelles. Mé v'chîn Bellérophon
êtchèrfroutchi ès clius, la touâle - mén êtalon.

METALLIC PEGASUS

Perched on the horns of the moon, I look at the brooks of lights,
a starry mirror of constellations below.
The black is dotted with diamonds of the gods,
a burning treasury, an inferno of finery.

Mercury, his ankles winged, does not run with such speed;
Neptune, the rising tide, does not sway the ocean
at the pace that I trample the air below the sky, over the earth -
my strides scythe the wraiths of the wind,

those horizon-runners, golden-scaled dragons
which weave the night. Each step of Pegasus's gallop
ignites lightning. The metal drips in twist-
ed paths that Vulcan forges from splashes of smoke and gas.

Wispy clouds are fragile. Here am I, Bellerophon,
astride storm-clouds, the whirlwind - my steed.

SHONA JOHNSON

I'm originally from Essex, but settled in Jersey in 2019.

My creativity usually comes from the darker parts of my experience, with prominent themes being mental illness, nature, and folklore. I enjoy horror fiction and think some of my poems reflect that, while others are more grounded in personal growth.

I enjoy the writing process, regardless of the final product.

RESPITE

the days become long again
and gradually I drift
back into my body
my senses alight
with the promise of spring

RUMINATION

at home in my bath
i unseam my skull
from nape to brow
i tip my head forward
and empty into soapy water
so i can sit in the dark
and think clearly for a while

SAD SWIMMING

I lose myself in a rush of cold water.
I close my eyes and immerse my head.
I move my body against the tide
and for a moment, I don't wish I were dead.

I am soothed by the dull throb and sway,
the sea pulsing against my ears.
For a moment, I am not this sad thing
and all the world and its grief disappear.

I imagine myself submerged,
I look to the surface, my back flush with the ocean floor.
For one precious moment, I am reminded to swim with this pain,
not to sink nor to ignore;
but to accept and to explore
the possibility that my life could mean something more
than drowning, disappointment, and this shit metaphor.

CARRION

They cut the air like shears,
stark against the murking sky.
A flurry of black shapes, cruel and centuries-old,
they bear a warning in their cry:

We will eat your dead
and steal your eggs,
and when there is no more ruined meat
we will stalk your lame and hunt your weak.

A thousand sooty feathers and clawing feet.
Always lurking, ever-creeping
that murder of little eyes and sharpened beaks.

SHEILA JONES

I trained in drama at the Royal Academy of Music and spent my career working in the arts as teacher, director, performer and administrator. I have come late to the art of writing poetry.

ERINACEUS EUROPAEUS

Nightly he dines in a blue bowl
Arriving regularly between 9 and midnight
Confident he will be served supper.

This starry night of the solstice
He does not dine alone
A second approaches – lover or rival?

As the hostess stares transfixed
The interloper bumper-cars the blue bowl
Round and around the patio.

Her hedgehog curls ball-like, holds fast,
Immovable. Thwarted, the uninvited guest
Chunters off into the dampening night.

The diner still in the blue bowl
Uncurls and munches on, unperturbed.

HAIKU

Friable compost
Kitchen waste, garden debris
Worms working wonders

THE PRINCE'S CONSORT

Each week she takes the bus to town.
A window seat at hedgerow height
displays the seasons
as the weeks roll by.

Winter and trees stand filigreed
against an ashen sky
while fallow furrows
sprout wayward daffodils.

Then spring and plastic covers
tight-stretch the Royals
like blousy barmaids in a local
pulling pints.

A single agapanthus
anticipates the summer
while campanula and fleabane
erupt from granite walls.

On autumn mornings seabirds
pummel the roadside verge
and old men, sitting separately,
natter like gaggling geese.

Along the coast where pastel
cod houses cluster up the hill
great-gran's newly-fashioned cottage

remembers its neighbour.

ALEXANDER LANGLOIS

I make many mistakes in life and hope that one day I will finally start to learn from them. In the meantime, I will continue to use them as inspiration to write the occasional poem.

However, one mistake I could never make is to fall out of love with the ocean. Gotta go - tide is rising!

COFFEE & CARROT CAKE

Coffee, carrot cake, cinnamon kisses,
Hints of laughter, glares and remisses.
Wrapped and coiled, drawn in nearer,
Waiting, watching, eyes on dearer.
Tiramisu and taming of red wine tumblers,
Feasting, fading, into deepest of slumbers.
Distance, denial, the devil like desire,
Unconscious becoming of the thoughtless martyr.
At least in these moments your presence is mine,
Tempting less ticking and more tampering with time.
Please make me a chapter, and less of a line,
In this novella of you and how your life is divine.

SURRENDERED

Forest of weeds continues to tangle,
Gasp for my breath as it ties my ankle.
Hazy silhouettes, things I thought I saw,
Juvenile fish obey juvenile law.

Tidal temptations draw me to the south,
The thought of being lost drying my mouth.
Overgrown rock beds, most vigilant hands,
Syringes and slashes quilted in sands.

From sunk and surrendered, to miles unknown,
Of creatures and beasts still yet to be shown.
Find what I look for, even in the depths,
Never know, only hope, for what comes next...

LOST

For someone who is lost,
I still refuse to be found.
My mind in the sky,
My heart underground.
I'm always what you need,
Never what you desire.
My mouth remains sealed,
My mind echoes like a choir.

Perhaps this is the beginning
Of an end I did not see -
The line when I grow old,
And you have no love for me?

But still I will fight,
For the memory of my dreams,
Even after what is left
Begins to break at the seams.
For the final time I repair,
And re-stitch my heart,
And find what I lost,
By going back to the start.

STANDSTILL

It has been a while, yet you're still on my mind,
I say I've moved on, yet true words I cannot find.
At a standstill I stay, until you find your way
To my side of which I'm blind, as my life begins to fray.
My thoughts they come, yet are destined to go,
In the words of an artist, to somewhere only we know.
What happened to the sequel we never got to read,
Did you ever think once, how much of you I need?

In a bubble you can stay, to where I should return,
But once the exit was passed, its frame began to burn.
I can't search for something I left long ago,
For in my mind you're the same, but my wrinkles now show.
I wonder, I plead, for your thoughts of me,
But like the sandman we know, I forever wait dreamily.

REMEMBER

Forget the time, tempers and joys,
Reminisce nothing, a vestige of white noise.

Forget the words, the paintings in rain,
The feelings of existence making us wane.

Remember the dreams, the ecstasy of moments,
Ephemeral they be, like their broken proponents.

Remember, to me, you're not so easily forgot,
The thought of you, an eternal forget-me-not.

JAMES
LE COCQ

I am a bookseller living in Jersey.

For my poetry, I take what people are saying around me, scramble the words and phrases, and combine them into new lines.

My goal is for readers to put their own unique impressions to my poems, and take from them what they personally see in each one.

PECCADILLOES (25/05/2022)

A mistake, a foible.
You hear it, you say it,
and see how many laugh.

Scrabble for calm,
Keep hold of your pancreas!
I've got crisps in case you collapse.

Pick the book up.
Turn off; withdraw
from this new-system drivel.

Eighteen poets,
the last guards for old words
sitting comfortably on cannabis buns,
larking with hearts in season.

Editor's Note:
The working title of this anthology was 'Peccadilloes' – would that excuse any typos
which managed to get past our perfectly pedantic proofreader Nick...?!

peccadillo
a small or venial fault or sin; a trifling offence
Oxford English Dictionary

STEFAN
LE MARQUAND

Born and raised in Jersey, I co-founded La Poèt'tie, before moving to London.

I learnt to apply myself to poetry during secondary school to express myself, I've always written from the heart and in the moment.

I'm reluctant to edit, staying true to myself, drawing inspiration from the mundane and bringing it to life in my mind.

THE BEGINNING

It is time
It is the beginning
Everything can happen
Everything is going to change
I'm all too aware of what will happen
Of everything that's going to appear
But nothing is going to be the same
As darkness begins to falter
It begins

Freedom to exposure
Freedom to light
Freedom to breathe
I have escaped, or rather was I
coerced
I am meeting life for the first time
And yet I see nothing
All I can see are colours, they're
bright
I can't open my eyes and I'm not
ready to see

They're taking me away
Am I not enough
Am I not ready
Did it all happen too soon
Questions are being flung left, right
and centre
Is this the beginning, or another end

Sleep now, bring it all back to
normality
Let us bring you back to familiar
homelands
Territory invaded
A life created
Changed and amended, a fresh
perspective

I can hear the relief in hushed
whispers
The longing of sleep and wishes of
health
Everything is going to be OK

I can reach out and feel the
sensations of skin
Everything is becoming too real now
There are tears being shed, there is
warmth
Love is present, I am...
I am alive, and yet, I cannot speak

I have dreamt, and I will dream again
I hope,
I do not understand, I must go back
I was not ready, but still I feel safe

Is this... who is this, that bears
me so close
I am... I am hungry

A HOMELY VIEW

They say; home is where the heart is
My Mum? Home is when the pictures get hung up.

Now explain this to me:
When *they* hammered one hundred picture hooks
Right through my heart
Was it comforting or was it simply settling
Was I your proverbial home or were you squatting

False senses of security lingered
But, maybe this was what you needed
Maybe I was doing you a service
Yeah, that would do, that was it

Now time to wash it away with tea
Or sink down into the water
Deep breath now, just relax
Because someday the cracks will show, and time will tell
Was I your house, or more your home?

Stand up, take stock, more tea
I see another out the windows
My eyes meet theirs, with a knowing smile
Try moving it to the right
Maybe a little more to the left?
Straighten it out, make sure it's level
Because if they're going to stay
They can ignore the Polyfilla speckled walls
And puncture it once more

Because so long as they put the pictures up
Then my heart will be their home.

MIND THE GAP

The darkness rolls
The windows open
The drifting chills
The silent souls
Crisp and clear
Nothing to see
"Mind the gap"

The rumble and cockle
The stone and steel
The call of robots
The stop and start
Faceless minds are drifting
Turning with pacified whispers
Another "Mind the gap"

The covering of blue fabrics
The drawing in of bodies
The surplus heat is growing
The dawn is slowly rising

Taken aback by another journey
Pushing through night after night
Last time "Mind the Gap"

The exit signs flicker
The untimely rushing air
The splashes of colour
The slow moving adverts
I can see daylight
Reminding me of purpose
No "Mind the gap"

The onward journey
The thick smog
The tireless beginning
The fiscal race
Time to jump
Faster and higher
"Mind the gap"

COBBLESTONE DRONES

The aimless buzz and
Mindless chatter;
Bumping face-to-face and
We're the same;
Sidestep, sashay and...

Target locked.
Guns blazing.
Rocketing around and
Sit down, and....

Coffee?
Sure thing, black, and
Duck down
Facial recognition activated,
Camouflage operational and
White noise engaged.
Amble on, back to the mission and

Evasive manoeuvres and
Music is blaring
Internal monologues daring and
Another collision, and...

Internally: "Do I know you...?" and
Fake it, make it, break it
Externally: "Oh! How's the family?" and
Suspicion detected
Jokingly: "Ah, well, this is awkward..." and
Abort mission, abort!

Safely returned to the comfort box and
Such is the life
Of you and I
The Cobblestone Drones

NOTHING

Let me ask you
When was the last time
Someone said that

You are,
You have,
Or, You mean,
Nothing?

Close your eyes
What do you see
The darkness? Nothing?

Try again, once more
Close your eyes
What do you see

Colours, words, shapes or form?
Thoughts, causes, sounds or
emotion?

Yourself, others, the past or the
future?

All of this
From that
Which was once
Nothing

Keep your eyes closed
There's more to see

All that you are?
All that you have?
All that you mean?

The Freedom to be
The Freedom to create
The Freedom to evoke

Now
Open your eyes
Do you see

That there is beauty
From that
Which was once

Nothing

SURROUNDING ME

Downward turned gaze
Lost in a musical haze
Experiencing and hearing
From the inside, jeering
As reflections pass by
The fires burning, I'll try
To show the world who
I can be, I want to be
Statuesque reminders, living
Moments of solace, unforgiving
Movement embodied, colours flying
People giving, simply trying
To be who they want to be
That was the Stonewall decree
And here I am, doing it for me.

HAMISH LEE

I am Hamish Lee, 70 yrs old.

My home town is Greenock in Scotland but I now live in Jersey. I went to The Mount Secondary School and was a soldier and then a railway signalman.

I've been writing since my first day in school because they made me.

I rest my case.

SURE PLAYS MEAN

Transferring our banking to Jersey,
as we entered the bank a Smooth Man
dressed in diplomatic efficiency asked if
he "could possibly help us"
Laura answered, "Sorry where?"
Bemused, Smooth Man just stared,
I hastily interjected,
"Sorry but my wife's eyesight is poor and
she has poor hearing so please be patient."
"Ah!" he said, understanding and smiling inanely.
He turned to Laura and told her,
"I'm so sorry to hear about your disabilities,
but we'll be able to work around your deficiencies."
And thus, he charged full tilt into the 'Death Zone.'
He asked if he "could possibly learn my name"
then he turned to Laura and with a raised voice,
almost shouting, he said "And you will be?"
Smiling guilelessly and in her sweetest voice she replied,
as sharply as the edge of a cut throat razor,
"The fucking Pinball Wizard".

Smooth man rolled smoothly away,
as if fleeing on wheels, and
a pleasant young lady took over.

EVOLUTION

1. Potted Possibilities

The mighty dinosaurs are dead
but their history from the shale is read,
bold epitaph for men to preach
of bones and beaks and claws and teeth.
Giant frothy fossil palms
are gathered up like beggars alms
and photographed and talked about
marked, measured and sorted out.
We've noted carefully whence they came
and given them each a fancy name,
our jigsawed knowledge missing bits
each piece a prize if we make it fit.
In science's mad exotic world
where sceptics challenge every word,
prophets preach against the bet
genetics can revive them - yet
what reception would they get
if dinosaurs lived today?
There would be stegosaur steaks
and bronty burgers
and sauropod soup
and brachio bagels
and trilobites with peas and chips
and ammonites chopped into little bits
all neatly boxed and priced
and that's what it would be like
if dinosaurs lived today.

EVOLUTION

2. Ug

Ug,
bored out of his skull
and tired of playing with his fingers,
sat rubbing two sticks together, waiting
for Mitochondrial Eve
to finish evolving her superior brain.

Evolving is a bit like washing your hair
but instead of using water you use DNA as shampoo
and genetics as conditioner.
And it takes longer,
but waiting was no problem for Ug,
he wasn't evolving any more anyway.

Next thing he knows, just as Eve shows up,
the sticks burst into flame
and there he is prancing about like a total wally,
beating the flames out of his reeking pelt,
with her standing, looking on, totally bemused.

Then Eve provides a demonstration of her superior brain
and tells him, "That's fire Ug,
we can cook on it and everything".
Ug says "Oh! Right, that'll be you finished evolving then will it?"
"I think so" she said, "for the moment anyway."
"Good" he said "then we can get on with inventing stuff"
then added, "Here, have a dollop of this fermented fruit,
I'll have a bit more and we'll see if it's poisonous".

This explains why women say stuff like
"I really don't think that's a good idea"
and men say stuff like
"I wonder what happens
if I hit it wiv a brick".

We might have come down from the trees
but we're not out of the woods yet.

EVOLUTION

3. Cro-Magnon

he wakes wild eyed
his mate whoops
what?
he would tell her
but they have no words

just cough
hello

grunt
food

growl
fight

screech
danger quick
climb a tree

but they have intellect
and understand concepts
he understands charcoal

taking her gently by the hand
he shambles hunch-backed
to their cave wall
where he places her palm
fingers spread
against the rock wall
and with charcoal draws around it

she stares at the shape of her
hand there
he places his own over it and
draws again

she understands
her
him
there on the rock wall
for all to see
for all time

the first love poem

WOMAN

I'm gonna find me a good time, rag time woman,
who moves like a lady, a loose limbed woman,
a smooth, svelte, slinkin', slidin', smokin' dream vision,
swinging hips, with red lips, a high steppin' woman.

Sequins on her dress shining under the spotlights,
a high heel, sling back, long leg eye catchin' woman,
made loosely then tightly in all the right places,
a high cheeked, fine featured, heart breakin' woman.

Never mind she got nothin' on hold but a smile,
I want her for mine, this bright, eyes blazin' woman,
her fingers plucking on the strings of my heart,
her heat throbbing in my head, I need that woman,
her hips grinding, arms slidin', embracing and holding,
so Lord make me bold so I claim this full time woman.

The woman's reply - see Laura Lee's poem 'Time'.

SPIRIT

Passing behind a group of German tourists being herded
into the town church by their guide,
I saw Ilene standing staring dully at them.
She saw me approach and broke into her usual mischievous smile.
"How ya doin'?" I asked her. "Oh, I'm all right" she replied
erupting in her usual cackling laughter.
"It's just them" she said and pointed to the tourists.
"Oh well" she sighed, "That was then and this is now.
I'll tell you though, their daddy's were buggers.
They stole our food and we went hungry.
And me, going to school in my bare feet.
When we were allowed we went down the beach
and picked limpets, cockles and mussels
and mum made us jelly with seaweed.
It was horrible, but what could you do?
It was that or starve and we were always hungry.
You know my friend's dad got caught with a radio.
He was deported and died in a prison camp.
And my dad was forced to work in the bakery they built.
How we cheered when the relief ships came.
We whistled and clapped when the soldiers came ashore
and waved the flags we had hidden from the Germans.
I'll give them one thing though -
when the bodies of our boys washed up on the shore
they got proper funerals with Union flags on their coffins.
No doubt they had their reasons,
maybe they thought it would soften us up.
They were wrong.
Anyway, there you are. Right,
I'm off, I've got shopping to do,
they're bringing round my new great-granddaughter
that's three you know. So I'll see you Sunday."
With that she was gone, joyously cackling like a harpy.
And with those departing steps
she walked proudly ahead of the past seventy five years,
laying down her own part in history,
head up, back straight, a woman,
a Jersey woman
proud and true.

CRITIQUE

Firmly he stated
"That's not poetry
that's doggerel!"
He had a full head of steam
and went at it with a vengeance.
I tuned him out
and while he waffled on
I thought about what he'd said.

It's well written I thought, but to be fair
the spelling's a bit dodgy.
But it's not comic verse
nor is it badly expressed and therefore
by definition,
it's not doggerel.

When his battery finally ran down
he said "Well!"
as if issuing a challenge.

I replied "It's not doggerel but here,
here's something for you to work with -
Woof!! Woof!!" I said,
and walked away.

LAURA
LEE

I am Laura Lee. Born in London and raised in Dundee.

Working in a Safari Park was where I enjoyed myself the most.

I have achieved my lifelong dream of touring Africa.

Now retired, I live in Jersey and enjoy painting and writing, both of which are a challenge because I suffer from impaired vision.

TIME

He found her dazzling in the moonlight
Everything about her was glowing, just right

Ruby red lips, smooth swinging hips
Love at first sight really exists

She caught his eye and instantly knew
What he felt, because she felt it too

Soft music played, they started to dance
This was the start of a real romance

He vowed to love her for the rest of his life
Forsaking all others makes her his wife

Their love for each other both true and strong
They didn't notice the years ticking on

Her long legs no longer run through the grass
Those slinky hips are now a fat arse

Her luscious red lips now narrow and thin
But a gorgeous young woman is hiding within

That lovely flamingo gave him her best
And over the years she gave him the rest

She feels love and hurt, joy and pain
Knowing her youth she'll never regain

She slowly wipes a tear from her eye
Remembering those wonderful years gone by

The love of her life comes wandering in
And suddenly she feels young again

Memories surface as music starts
He asks "Care to dance my little sweetheart?"

She struggles a bit getting out of her chair
Straightens her dress then pats her hair

He closes his eyes and can clearly see
His beautiful woman as she used to be

That long ago moonlight, silvery shone
A beacon of love to go on and on

As the dark of the night turned into day
They held each other tight then flew away

This was written in response to Hamish Lee's poem 'Woman'.

FRUIT

Fruit is used in many ways
Sometimes it's used in displays

Think of all the things we make
Smoothies, ice pops, pies and cake

Blend it, bake it, freeze and stew
Even stick it on the BBQ

When a guy thinks a girl is cute
He'll describe her using names of fruit

Like a Peach her skin is smooth and fair
With locks of Strawberry Blonde hair

Her lips are like Cherries ripe
Sweet to taste, a pure delight

She is the Apple of his eye
But she is in love with another guy

He knows right away this guy he hates
But it's just a case of sour Grapes

She is his darling Clementine
He wishes their hearts could intertwine

After all this time he loves her still
But he now sits alone on Blueberry Hill

These fruits we've tried from time to time
Pineapple, Grapefruit, Lemon and Lime

There's more exotic if you dare
Papaya, Pawpaw and Prickly Pear

Dragon Fruit, Egg Fruit, Star Fruit and Plum
Lychee and Mango many more to come

With such a large choice you could go tropicana
But I think I'll stick with a simple Banana

MY PLACE

Perception of place
It's really just an empty space

Ask me, "is it here or is it there?"
But it isn't really anywhere

I paint a picture in my mind
I can erase it at any time

The sense of touch is quite unique
From the top of your head to the soles of your feet

You might get a nice surprise
If you link together ears and eyes

When mixing together sight and sound
You get a clearer picture all around

Then we have our taste and smell
They work together very well

With taste you'll get both sour and sweet
Add sense of smell, it works a treat

Use all these things to fill your space
Then the empty space becomes a place

THAT'S MY GIRL

She luxuriated on the bed
He sat down beside her
Their eyes met
Her bright yet loving gaze melted his heart
He gently stroked her golden mane
She stretched in ecstasy
He walked to the door
Without being asked she joined him
When the door opened she went on ahead
"Wait for me" he called
Together they went for a walk
One man and his dog

THE MAMMOTH AROUND MY NECK

In a frozen land all on their own
Giant woolly mammoths roam

On a land of ice and mountains high
Mammoths live and mammoths die

Fresh grazing was in great demand
So, they journeyed south to Doggerland

Temperatures rose as the climate changed
Snow melted away more grazing gained

Melting ice caused the oceans to rise
This was the start of the mammoth's demise

The North Sea formed and the seas did expand
Surrounding their island and invading their land

A shrinking island and fresh water low
The mammoths had nowhere else to go

As their island continued to shrink
With nothing to eat and nothing to drink

The mammoths all died and fell to their knees
They lay undiscovered for centuries

Seven and a half thousand years have passed
The woolly mammoth breathed their last

Entombed in mud, ice and clay
They lay undisturbed to the present day

Too late now for anyone to save
They rot and decay in a watery grave

That watery grave where monsters did fall
Became disturbed by fishermen's haul

Numerous tusks were hauled from the depths
Witnessing their tragic deaths

Hues of cream, tan and chocolate brown
Preserved as they were when they went down

From the ice and water and the depths of time
To the grasping trawl of a fisherman's line

Like the long-ago men who cut and carved
To the jeweller who cut and trimmed and shaved

The history of those ancient days I can hold
Trimmed and polished and bound in gold

To secure the memory so I may reflect
On the mammoth I wear around my neck

JUDY
MANTLE

I was born and brought up in Jersey and am now seventy-six.

After studying and teaching in England, France and Canada, I returned
to the island in 1979.

I have been writing for as long as I can remember.

My interests include swimming, travel and meeting with friends.

I am the proud mother of three children and have three
young granddaughters.

HARE

(on the Roman road at Pont St Jacques, Brittany)

How huge he is, the hare
who sits there, stares,
seems to question who I am,
why here, on this path,
sharing his space
uninvited.

I had imagined hares to be
like rabbits but with pricked up ears,
No, he's the size
and as wide eyed as a young fawn.
He fixes me with amber glare,
unafraid.

Romans brought hares north they say.
Could be why he claims this place
with such authority? His forebears lope,
like him, cleave fields and hills
make this their home,
unquestioned.

SMALL WORLDS

This is the beach where I grew up, learnt to swim
nearly drowned, watched my nut-brown father
home on leave, walk on his hands
along the water's edge, his path traced
by wet indentations in the sand.

That granite crag, our Peak in Darien
I recognise each handhold, plateau, cleft
but where my small foot found a perfect fit
there is no space for feet the size of mine.

Grandchildren search for shells and fish for shrimps
in pools which seemed so bottomless to me
I close my eyes and shrink to share their view
feel seaweed fronds wrap round my heels
to peel back all the years from then to now.

This poem was placed 1st in the Channel Islands Category of the 2019 Guernsey International Poetry Competition.

EBB AND FLOW

We islanders are never shocked
to feel the force of an ebbing tide
tug at our legs to pull us back.

The tide is going out so fast
that sea fern, bubbles, little leaves
scud past me as I swim for shore.

The varnished surface, glazed and smooth
belies the rip that runs beneath
and tries to carry me to France.

Shall I lie back, float, let go
and let this current take me there,
see where the ripples let me lie?

THE TWO KAYS

(who missed one another by 23 days)

I watched you shrinking
daily,
hurting all over
breath coming shorter, laboured gasps,
moving less and less and less,
but mind and eyes still wide alive;
you growing smaller and thinner
me, heavier and fatter
you, in almost death as in life,
so brave, uncomplaining
your humour intact
waiting to die.

Meanwhile,
your granddaughter,
my wondrous dancing star daughter,
circus girl
was growing daily
in utero,
kicking and shoving, moving to music,
practicing her trapeze acts even then,
waiting to be born.

You two kindred spirits...
if only you had met.

R.I.P.

There are so many poems in the Poetry Hospital
brought in with sirens blaring, needing care
then left on trolleys in crowded corridors
until their maladies are diagnosed
and treatments recommended. Removal
of deep-seated metaphors, amputation
of loose-limbed clichés, excision of adverbs,
abstract nouns and excessive alliteration,
chemotherapy to eradicate illogical line
breaks. ITU doctors shake their heads
agree there is no hope. Withdraw all treatment.

On clipboards at the foot of all beds
printed in bold black ink

DO NOT RESUSCITATE

NICK POINGDESTRE

I've never been a great reader of poetry but enjoy the occasional foray into that world. I like the form mostly as entertainment.

My own poems are predominantly inspired by people or events and I like to instill some humour or wry observation into them.

I also appreciate poems as art but this higher level of poetry is somewhat beyond my ability. My burger and chips to your filet mignon!

ON THE STROKE OF THREE

"There's no such thing as ghosts"
Mother had said
But I'm not so sure
Now that she's dead

She suddenly went
On the stroke of three
We'd always had a notion
That that's when it would be

Because strokes one and two
Were never in doubt
As everyone knows –
Three strokes and you're out

So here we are with a
Shadow of a doubt
Has she passed over?
Or is she hanging about??

There's a miasma in
The atmosphere
A whiff of Yardley
Scents the air

In bed I pull the covers up tight
I would never sleep

If I turned out the light
And as I cower underneath
I hear her voice,
"Did you brush your teeth?"

It didn't take her long to
Have a moan
And now she doesn't even
Need a phone
I sense her presence everywhere
A second gin? I wouldn't dare!

The astral pull holds no sway
Mother just doesn't want to go
that way!
Her beady eyes are fixed on me
She purses her lips on the strike
of three

We both know now
It's a waiting game
When I dream she's calling my name
I know she's preparing a
heavenly tea
It will be me and her for eternity

ADIOS COVID

We're nearly there with this Covid crap
Studiously reviewed that exit map
Patiently queued for inoculation
So that we can have a summer vacation

The reservations are made to do our hair
It's a little longer than it was last year
The nails and lashes have both been done
We're nearly ready for some summer sun

There's just one fly in the sunshine ointment
Like most lockdown ladies there's a huge disappointment
Our waistlines show the error of our ways
Of eating like pigs in those lazy lockdown days
(Oink, oink!)

INDECISION

For twenty-three years we've been together
And now I've reached the end of my tether
It wasn't too bad right at the start
But now all he does is burp and fart

How I scream when we watch television
He flicks the remote with such indecision
Will it be football? Will it be cricket?
Try changing the channel where I want to stick it

He reclines like a king and I'm just a drudge
Give me a taser and I'll make him budge
Or crack a lasso around his ears
When he commands the drudge to bring him his beers

He watches the screen and I watch his face
How it would crumple if I sprayed it with mace
And as I sit there just by his side
I smile sweetly planning mariticide

And so in my head I go over the choices
Then once again I hear those voices
I place both my hands to the sides of my head
"You'll never get peace until he's dead"

He's in control and I'm losing my mind
I want to destroy all of *man*kind
But God moves in mysterious ways
And the madness is gone with my Songs of Praise

THE NONCHALANT COW

The nonchalant cow sits quite demure
Can't even be bothered to make manure
To chew some grass doesn't enter her mind
She'd much rather flatten it with her fat behind

A funny looking tourist then cycles past
If it's the Tour de France he's definitely last
Yells out "Moo Moo" but she's not impressed
She won't consort with the improperly dressed

Now here comes the farmer, all wellies and muck
With the cattle prod and that unspeakable truck
But when she thinks of it, Oh! Does she shudder
That indecent thing he does with her udder

NICKI

Oh dear Nick what a tragic end
Not only of a colleague but also a friend
There was still so much more to say
It's now too late to save for another day

It was always "Hello Darling" and a wave in the street
Then the quickening pace of those busy feet
Impatient to hear tales of sex and booze
Well its goodbye dear Nick, for, sadly, today you're the news

ALEXANDER VAUDIN RICE

I have been writing for the best part of forty years and was encouraged to write poetry by Alan Jones at Hautlieu School who included some of my work in the school publication 'High Places'.

My family has played a huge role in my writing.

I have benefitted greatly from being a member of La Poèt'tie and The Heather View Writers.

BAJAN DREAM

That little frog
white: translucent almost
caged in the thick of a wine glass:

freshness,
monsoon rains
must have spurred them on,
myself the fairy tale frog
rejected by his princess.
That ring, so neatly proffered
one knee down –
an ill-advised question
unnecessary to one content
with how things are.

Helpful to have the harsh carapace of the turtle
slowly swimming around
the flying hobie cats
manned by the black Bajan crew
confident: standing them up to crest the waves
and glide through rising foam.

Later to sit in the sun
and raise a glass of rum and coke
as friends warmly converse
the sun sets on a Bajan dream.

I DROP A TENNER

I leave a tenner on the beach
It scurries across the sand
I catch it like a crab.
Money like a tide dribbles over me
A spume of coins...

Geld strips me of my meaning.

A sea populated by hermit crabs
Has no need
Or takes no heed
Of Geld, spondulicks
Or plump wonga.

Coins and notes
Brag of their value –
Lead us to the safe havens
Such as mortgages and banks' investments
Which kill our souls
And the brightest of our dreams.

The hermit crabs
Just shed their shekel shells
And start again.

Geld is the German word for money.

HEMINGWAY AND CIGARS

Celebrate Che Guevara, El Comandante!
In Revolutionary Square the outline
Of his face imprints a building.
In the back of a Russian Lada
We return to our hotel
Breathing in
The deadly fumes of every gear change.
A crucifix hangs from the rear-view mirror.
I cross myself as we return safely, greeted
By laughter from fellow guests.

Unlimited curiosity by tourists and locals alike;
We bring currency, medicines and tales of the outside world.
They may travel abroad, with limitations,
Having a year's wage to spare.

Baseball is the national sport, left behind
By the Americans with the cars lovingly restored!
The Hotel Nacional a former playground
For Hemingway and his friends.

Always music wherever you go, salsa, merengue – mojitos and cigars.
It's an ongoing fiesta as ageless as the Buena Vista Social Club.
And the sun sets with a tribute to the people's hero: El Comandante.

LOST AND FOUND

They say, "nothing is ever lost"...

It belongs to a Special Poet.
A blue gilet and he left it behind
At the pub last night...

Smooth to the touch of cheek it reminds me of a Comfort Blanket...
The scent of hours of performance in pubs and other venues.

Alliteration and assonance
Embedded in its fibres and I am Happy that I brought it here

Given custody.

I also brought home a wooden walking stick
Belonging to another Special Poet.
I garnered a friendly response
As, Distinguished, I walked along confidently stick in hand.

Now that both items have been collected and recollected
I sit here feeling naked,
Propless,
A slightly nervous speaker
Of my own work –
I have much to do

THE OLIVE TREE

Once two trees fighting for space became one,

Six hundred years old.

Full of knots,

A trunk like arms and legs

Bonded, a sculpture.

Revered old wood resting silently.

Leaves flourish from this ancient, ageless stump.

Bearing fruit.

Hollow and yet still growing.

Fresh shoots rise.

The trunk in the colour of grey bread.

Silver leaves in the glow of the full moon.

BEN
SPINK

I may be biased, but I believe Jèrriais is extraordinarily beautiful.

I started learning in 2018 and was instantly hooked. I have never felt so at home with a language, as if I've tapped into a fundamental part of my soul!

I love the playfulness and rich earthiness of Jersey's native tongue, which lends itself perfectly to children's poetry.

LA MAUVAISE MAUVE

Nou dit qu'oulle est totchie,
ou 'tait à m'nichi

Touos les gens sus la grève
auve sa dgiâbliéthie,

D'abord, i's'n allaient
endormi la mauve,

Mais les gens dîtent,
'Nou-fait! I' faut sauver chutte pauvre.'

Ch'est-i' un forfait d'chiper un chapé?
Ch'est-i' si mauvais d'bétchie une beurrée?

Pourtchi la punni pouor un mio d'mêché?
Pourtchi forbanni chutte mauve affrontée?

Ou gobe tchiques frites,
véthe, ou gaffe des macarons,

Toutefais, ou n'a tué pèrsonne,
n'oubliez pon!

Achteu, malheutheusement,
ou d'meuthe ès Mîntchièrs,

Où'est qu'ou joue, solitaithement,
parmi les rotchièrs.

THE SAVAGE SEAGULL

They say it's crazy,
it was menacing

All the people on the beach
with its devilry,

At first, they were going
to put the gull to sleep,

But the people said,
"No way! We have to save the poor thing."

Is it so bad to pinch a hat?
Is it a crime to peck a sandwich?

Why punish it for a bit of mischief?
Why banish this cheeky seagull?

It snatches some chips,
true, it grabs macaroons,

However, it hasn't killed anyone,
don't forget!

Now, unfortunately,
it lives on the Minquiers,

Where it plays, solitarily,
amongst the rocks.

I' TCHAIT D'LA PLYIE

Man doue d'la vie
I' tchait d'la plyie
Touos les jours, toutes les nyits
I' tchait d'la plyie

Quand jé m'sis rêvilyi
I' tchiyait d'la plyie
Quand j'm'en vais m'couochi
I' tchèrra d'la plyie

I' tchait des cats
I' tchait des tchians
I' tchait des crapauds
Dé temps en temps!

La s'maine pâssée
Et la s'maine tchi veint
I' tchiyait hièr,
I' tchèrra d'main

I' tchit à verse et
I' tchit hardi
Chu jour dé tchi
tch'i' tchit tant d'plyie

IT'S TIPPING WITH RAIN

Oh what a fright
It's tipping with rain
Every day, every night
It's tipping with rain

When I lifted my head
It was tipping with rain
When I go to bed
It'll be raining again

It's raining cats
It's raining dogs
From time to time
It's raining ~~frogs~~ toads!

The week just past
And the week that'll follow
It rained yesterday
It'll rain tomorrow

It chucked it down
It poured with rain
That day the rains came
again and again

PAM
TREHIOU

Joining a writing group after retiring from teaching, I found creating and reading my poems difficult at first as many were personal. I had to be brave, learnt a lot by listening, discussing and rewriting.

As a photographer, poems often start with what I see. I like to write poems that have something to say, I'd describe them as very eclectic!

DEMENTIA

1.

You have lived so long and learnt so much
yet can't recall thoughts flashing by
Memories ebb and flow
Words
      dance
             before you
  myriads of light
          falling
            like
              grains of sand

Soon lost within the tides of time
confused beyond your concept
forgetting the places you want be
you wander through life

Yet there are glimpses of delight
like hidden pearls
circling around your mind

Do you listen to tunes
you loved to sing
          magical birdsong
                  rainbow days
You move slowly
living out each day
in a maze
seeking a way out

Still you stand

DEMENTIA

2.

As the light shines through the clouds
As life changes
And memories grow dim
The sun sets
But it is always there
As you are
The same but fading away
Through the darkness

Sometimes the memories are flawed
But like the cracks
They do not separate just become linear
Unconnected
Memories bend like the light to reveal you
A different you but always you
Don't be sad because there is always
That crack of light

MYSTICAL TOR

1. Glastonbury Tor

Standing alone. So majestic. Centuries old.
Solitary guardian of all that nature has created.
Centuries and cultures meeting on your lines.
The muse of young and old coming together,
Hearts touching through hands and minds.
Bonds formed like interlocking boughs,
Dependent on each other,
Supporting and growing in spirit,
Trying to unravel your mysteries.
Many people looking for answers,
Trying to break the chains of materialism,
Fighting for freedom, the right to choose,
Hope soaring into the unknown.
How many changes have you seen?
How many more changes
Must you allow to go unchallenged?

MYSTICAL TOR

2. Summer Solstice

The primeval, haunting sound of the didgeridoo
Drifts in the midsummer air,
Until it blends with the sweet-piercing violins
Soaring from the ruins of Arthur's Camelot.
The music meanders along the ancient leylines,
Rising and falling with the ebb and flow of the levels,
Allowing mystical hopes to soar into the moonlit sky.

FAIRMILE '97

twenty-four months side by side
lawyer pensioner
security guard housewife
child in the push chair
hippy and artist
building homes
of wood and canvas
high in top branches
trapeze artists swung
on wire thin ropes suspended
amongst the stand of ancient oaks
they waited in darkness
flinching at shadows
lighting fires to keep
away nightmares
hiding in a maze
of tunnels woven
between time-worn roots
they stopped machines
as chained they waited
congregating in circles
they sang songs
wrote poems
shouted obscenities
at yellow topped hats
muddied black boots
aggression driven
without orders
advancing relentlessly
a world devoured
driven by a monster
thick and black
now our future moves
along the tarmacadam
cars thrum along trunk roads
travellers hurrying

LOVE LUST

Wake up my heart, get out of bed,
why did you sleep so long?
Your musky smell invades my head,
Why does it feel so wrong?
A careless thought is all it took,
a whispered word - a simmering look,
to discard clothes - let passion win!
No rational thoughts just skin to skin.
Light begins to pierce the gloom,
a one-night stand, a hotel room
where bedclothes lay, a tangled heap
And what we sow, so shall we reap.
Outside the world is full of song,
I shout the words I should have said -
Get up you fool, get out of bed,
you've been with me too long!

SHATTERED

scattered shivers   snaking crevasses
tumbling trembling   icy fingers
                    a cacophony sounds
waves pillow   white water
cascading through   seething foam
beaded droplets   of skipping pearls
whistling majestic   yet suspended
                    dancers fall into
bottomless oceans   silvery water
                as the earth evolves
                into shattered slivers

After a performance of the production 'Scattered' by dance-circus company
Motionhouse, at the Jersey Opera House.

JANE WAKEHAM

Sadly Jane passed away in 2020. She enthralled us with poetry ranging from William Shakespeare to Maya Angelou to Lemn Sissay, as well as her own writing. Her performance as Ophelia, to Geraint Jennings' Oberon in Jèrriais, is still a highlight of our past meetings.

Thanks to Jane's executors, Jane and Michael Churchill Blackie, for submitting these poems.

IT

(In memory of my dear, darling mother who died on November 12th 2010)

It, raped my mother. It had no respect.
Not embarrassed to execute this malevolent act
While I watch, a voyeur,
To
My dear, darling mother's damning demise.

It was measured, deliberate. It took its time.
Ten years or so and all the while
Embezzling her of the future and her past
And
I saw my dear, darling mum diminishing before my eyes.

It ravished her, left a shell.
An empty space, a beautiful face,
Where once life lived with such vitality
And
I saw my dear, darling mum declining before my eyes.

It, consumed my mother.
Alzheimer's burgled her brain, dementia destroyed her existence.
And
Peaceful at last, no battles left to fight
I cradled my dear, darling mum, in my arms

And she died...

THE LAST BREATH

Do not take that final breath.
Keep it for another day
Open your eyes and smile,
Tell me you love me
But
Today there must be no death.

Do not take that final breath.
Hold it in abeyance now
Sit up, talk, crave a cup of tea,
So I can tell you that I love you
But
Today there must be no death.

Do not take that final breath.
Let us stall time
Stop still and wait forever,
Hold my hand as I hold yours
But
Today there must be no death.

Today, there will be death.
My selfish wants
A mother's selfless love
Heaven awaits the shattered spirit
And
You take your final breath

ONE MORE TIME

One more breath.....

        Just one more.....

              So I can say I love you one more time.

One more breath.....

        Just one more.....

              So I can say thank you one more time.

One more breath.....

        Just one more.....

Make it last one more moment.....

        One more minute.....

              One more lifetime.....

So I can thank you and tell you that I love you one more time.

FOUR BY TWO

Waiting, solitary, surrounded by so many.
Waiting, feeling so forlorn.
Ahead, the unknown and feeling so alone.
I walk with fortitude to the beech door
Behind which holds my destiny like a dam.
The floodgates, will they open and my life flow away.

One lump, four by two he says.
Take them both doesn't bother me
Just get rid whatever do it
Wry smiles and no we won't do that.

A week later I lie on a bed
An art class of black arrows defining the guilty breast
And waiting solitary, surrounded by so many.
Surgery once, twice, chemo and radio
And in an instant my world is changed
Ahead the unknown and feeling so alone.

Three years on, nearly four,
Waiting, solitary, surrounded by so many.
Every day waiting for Breast Cancer not to return
Every day living, every day life!

JANE WARREN

Childhood was enriched with stories, both books and family anecdotes. My mother read poems to me when I was five.

Then followed decades of inhibitions against any creative writing, except for an occasional comic verse – one addressed to my bank manager.

A trip to Antarctica and two weeks in Sicily cured this and I have been writing poetry for nine years.

THE DANCE OF SPRING

The first of March is called the start of spring,
But now upon our ever-warming planet
Nature's impatient to begin the dance.

So will the moves of insects, plants and birds still stay in step
While daffodils, the Lenten lilies, like little yellow lanterns light the way
Gracing the grey, dull days of February with golden joy;
And earlier each year unseasonal warmth
Awakens bumble bees from their long winter's sleep
To fly in quest of nectar from the nearest snowdrop?

So by the vernal equinox all life is quickening.
At dawn the sun projects a path of gold into the prehistoric mound,
This is the vital signal that told our ancestors the light is gaining ground.
The trees know this: their sap is rising.
Their twigs and branches have a pinkish tinge
As buds appear that soon will burst in leaf.

The birds show this. The longer light alerts the rooks
To fly with sticks to renovate their rough and ready nests.
Well lined with moss and down, the little wren's more delicate creation
Provides a safe repository for eggs - the future generation.
The robin, that fiercely territorial bird, allows his mate
Raising their brood, to share his real estate.

And soon the dizzy dance, la primavera, is in full swing,
The air is full of birdsong, bees and butterflies
And happiness and hope. For now it's spring.

A FIELD IN SICILY
(Inspired by a visit in April, 2013)

Clear in the distance snow-capped Etna smoulders, fuming.
Nearer, a grove of olive trees, grey green leaves glimmering.
Closer again a meadow, long grass and wild flowers blowing.
Then the line of white stones where I am standing.

They bear the names of soldiers, British men,
Whose age suggests they fought and fought again,
In Africa perhaps. By nineteen forty-four
Most had fought through the first five years of war,
Earned their degrees in comradeship and courage,
Borne witness to catastrophe and carnage.
Now there was hope of victory and survival.

Then, for these men here, all fighting had to cease.
I thank them for over sixty years of peace,
Wish that I'd spent those years more fully, day by day,
Having been granted far more time than they.

Some were from Scotland, Durham, Hampshire, Jersey.
They lie now in this rich earth of Sicily,
Where once Phoenician vied with Greek,
Carthage fought Rome, then Normans came to seek
More land and power. Much later, Garibaldi
Landed his Redshirts: his quest Italian unity.
But these men here, our boys, came to free Europe.
So much blood shed through centuries to gain this ground;
Their names harder to read now, with wet eyes, I found.

Here in these graves young British soldiers lie
Where so many armies have trod.
Most named with their rank and their regiment
And then some known only to God.

THE PLEASURES OF FANTASY AND REALITY

The joyous sunshine of a Venetian June smiles on me where I sit
Sipping chilled rosé from a long stemmed glass,
I'm dressed in crisp white trousers and a black designer-knit
Watching with idle interest as the people pass.
Delicious Parma ham upon my plate
And green Italian sandals on my feet,
To have a witty man here as my date
Is all I need to make my bliss complete.
Instead to art I'll go and pay obeisance
And lose myself inside the High Renaissance.

In fact, it is October and in my garden, strutting proudly,
Resplendent, a cock pheasant trumpets his arrival loudly.
In Jersey, these game birds are protected
So there's no fear this month he'll be selected
In someone's sights to make up half a brace,
He can quite safely maintain his regal pace
Making a Royal Progress past my shrubs and brambles
And then next door continue on his rambles.

Indoors, I cease to watch his kingly capers
And turn to my green desk, awash with papers.
Clear autumn sunshine lights upon such ills
As broker's notes, old bank statements and bills.
I read them briefly while I suck a toffee
Then drink a strong black Ethiopian coffee.
Today I'm in no mind-set for the "loss" word:
Instead I'll lose myself inside the crossword.

IN DEFENCE OF DANDELIONS

1. Herbs Not Weeds

In days gone by when men cut grass with scythes,
Before the upkeep of a lawn replaced religion,
So many plants we now condemn as weeds
Were valued for their herbal properties,
And people then would pull away the grass
To help a dandelion to spread, for it was prized,
Not only for its lion's teeth leaves
Which still today we sometimes eat in salads,
But also for the yellow dye from its bright flowers
As well as for its root's medicinal powers.

Chickweed and camomile were cherished too,
And have we now forgotten a dock leaf's cooling balm
When pressed against an angry nettle's sting?
And that those self-same nettles when caught young
Can furnish tender leaves to cook and eat
And can be brewed for beer or drunk as tea?

For now, when zealots view a lawn
All must comply with grass conformity.
Daisies are seen as dangerous by these despots,
Insurgents with no chance to make a chain,
And dandelions are cast as villains of the piece.
Indeed it's war: there is no thought of peace.
Sometimes today to dodge this persecution
They grow far shorter stems: but all to no avail.

Continued overleaf

Yet once this vibrant plant was viewed as magical,
For herbalists could see its astral symbolism.
As first it was a golden sunlike disc,
Its spreading petals opening with the dawn
And closing at the setting of the sun.
Then, in the twinkling of an eye it seemed
Changed by the moon into a silver sphere
Translucent, pale, made up of tiny shooting stars
That on the breeze then travelled far afield.

And now, this star, this dandelion,
Once of the herbal hierarchy a pillar,
Today is outlawed and pursued
By horticultural Stasi wielding weed killer.

IN DEFENCE OF DANDELIONS

2. Face to Face

Today for the first time I really looked at a bright yellow dandelion:
Not on my lawn but in a neighbour's flowerbed
At my eye level as I walked down the hill,
Its tiny petals creating a glorious golden sunburst.
I thought, suppose these plants were rare
Brought back by some explorer from Peru,
Would we then value them and see them grown at Kew?
Do we despise all things that we have in abundance
Until their loss makes us regret this view?

Now *Sumer is icumen in* but there is no *cuccu**.
The chirpy house sparrow enjoying its dust-bath
Was thought too common once upon a time
Until we learned its numbers were badly in decline.
These dandelions have not the height and grace of daffodils,
They cannot dance and have no trumpets to sound their praises
So Wordsworth did not write about a host of golden dandelions.
But they are bright and beautiful and full of life and joy,
If all their clocks were stopped would we then cherish them?

---

* Reference thirteenth century 'Cuckoo Song' (anon)
Summer has come, loudly sing, cuckoo!

PARTING WITH PAINTINGS
OR THE PLAYBOY'S LAMENT

I'm down to my last Canaletto
The Rembrandts have both had to go,
Through trying to please a
False Mona Lisa
My furniture's out in the snow.

My first wife had all the Picassos
These partings are hard to avoid,
My second took both of the Tissots
Now my mistress has fled with the Freud.

Last Friday I fell for a red-head,
She said she was mad about art,
We were getting along
But the Turner has gone,
So I fear she was merely a tart.

The blond in the art shop was friendly,
So I asked her back home for a drink.
When she saw the Van Gogh
Her knickers fell off,
But she said "I am not what you think".

The raven-haired girl at the checkout
Said Monet was all she desired,
But I think I heard wrong
For my credit card's gone
And they say at the store she's retired.

Despite the Pre-Raphaelites' frolics,
For me paintings and women don't mix,
If I'd kept them apart
Or just stuck to art,
I'd never have been in this fix.

WITH SPECIAL THANKS TO:

All the contributors to this anthology who rose to the challenge and filled these pages with poems.

Each poet and appreciator of poetry who has attended, listened, shared and discussed with us such a variety of poetry, in many languages - including Anglo Saxon on the evening we celebrated our first anniversary.

Paul Craig and Neil Molyneux for their loyal support from the very beginning.

Société Jersiaise, namely former President Neil Molyneux and current President Nicolette Le Quesne Westwood, for inviting us to take up home in the comfort of the Members' Room, on the last Wednesday evening of each month.

Jersey Library for providing the perfect meeting space for our second Wednesday evening of the month discussion and feedback meetings - especially Marco, Pam, Helen and Cathy.

Jersey Festival of Words for immersing us in literature, particularly the poetry, and their support of La Poèt'tie.

Paul John Kilshaw for his original artwork which adorns the cover of this book.

Proofreader Nick Poingdestre for scrutinising the manuscript with such precision.

Our kind and generous sponsors Highvern and David Hart.

Richard Cornick and the team at Bigwoods Premier Printers Limited for producing this little book of big dreams.

And finally, co-founder Stefan Le Marquand for igniting inspiration.

JULIETTE HART
La Poèt'tie